My First Eucharist

W9-BZD-799

Place my picture here.

_____
(name)

_____
(date)

at

_____
(name of church)

Celebrating Our Faith

Eucharist

Principal Program Consultant
Dr. Jane Marie Osterholt, SP

BROWN-ROA
A Division of Harcourt Brace & Company

Nihil Obstat
Rev. Richard L. Schaefer

Imprimatur
✠ Most Rev. Jerome Hanus, OSB
Archbishop of Dubuque
August 21, 1998
Feast of Pope Saint Pius X
Patron of First Communicants

The Ad Hoc Committee to Oversee the Use of the Catechism, National Conference of Catholic Bishops, has found this catechetical series to be in conformity with the *Catechism of the Catholic Church*.

The nihil obstat and imprimatur are official declarations that a book or pamphlet is free of doctrinal or moral error. No implication is contained herein that those who granted the nihil obstat and imprimatur agree with the contents, opinions, or statements expressed.

BROWN-ROA
A Division of Harcourt Brace & Company

Our Mission

The primary mission of BROWN-ROA is to provide the Catholic markets with the highest quality catechetical print and media resources. The content of these resources reflects the best insights of current theology, methodology, and pedagogical research. These resources are practical and easy to use, designed to meet expressed market needs, and written to reflect the teachings of the Catholic Church.

Copyright © 2000 by BROWN-ROA, a division of Harcourt Brace & Company

All rights reserved. No part of this publication may be reproduced or transmitted in any form or by any means, electronic or mechanical, including photocopy, recording, or any information storage and retrieval system, without permission in writing from the publisher.

Requests for permission to make copies of any part of the work should be mailed to: Permissions Department, Harcourt Brace & Company, 6277 Sea Harbor Drive, Orlando, Florida 32887-6777.

Photography Credits
Cover: Stained-glass windows at Zimmerman Chapel, United Theological Seminary, Dayton, Ohio. Photography by Andy Snow Photographics.
Art Resource: National Museum of American Art: 73(c); **Gene Plaisted/The Crosiers:** 74;
Digital Imaging Group: 10, 18, 23, 26, 27, 34, 42, 50, 51, 54, 63, 66, 67, 76, 77, 78, 79, 80;
FPG International: Kevin Laubacher: 14; Arthur Tilley: 30; Dick Luria: 46; **John Barr/Gamma Liaison International:** 58; **Jack Holtel:** 7; **PhotoEdit:** David Young-Wolff: 38; Tony Freeman: 62;
Andy Snow Photographics: 11, 19, 31, 35, 39, 55, 59, 75; **Superstock:** 72, 73(bl); **Tony Stone Images:** Daniel Bosler: 6; Bruce Ayres: 22; **Jim Whitmer:** 47. Special thanks to the parish communities at St. Charles Borromeo, Kettering; St. Paul's, Oakwood; and Holy Angels, Dayton, for cooperation with photography.

Illustration Credits
Biblical Art: Chris Vallo/The Mazer Corporation: 8–9, 16–17, 24–25, 32–33, 40–41, 48–49, 56–57, 64–65; **Children's Art:** 12–13, 20–21, 28–29, 36–37, 44–45, 52–53, 60–61, 68–69 (prepared by Chelsea Arney, Lisol Arney, Kaley Bartosik, Hannah Berry, Noah Berry, Morgan Brickley, Brittany King, Cecily King, Jackie Malone, Katie Malone, Bob Ninneman, Claudia Ninneman, Erica Ninneman, Laura Grace Ninneman, Brittany Smith, Lauren Vallo, Ryan Vallo, and the art classes of Holy Angels School, Dayton)

Printed in the United States of America

ISBN 0-15-950447-3

20 19 18 17 16 15 14 13

Celebrating Our Faith

Eucharist

My First Communion

I will receive
Holy Communion
for the first time
during the celebration of the Eucharist
on

_____
(date)

at

_____.
(name of church)

I ask my family, my godparents,
my teacher, my classmates, my friends,
and everyone in my parish community
to help me prepare for this celebration.

_____
(signed)

Here are the signatures of people who are helping
me prepare for my First Communion.

A Blessing for Beginnings

"I am the bread that gives life!
No one who comes to me will ever be hungry."

—*John 6:35*

Leader: Today we gather to continue your journey of
initiation
as you prepare for First Communion.
We are ready to learn from one another
and from our Church community.
And so we pray:
God our Father, accept our thanks and praise for
your great love.
Jesus, Son of God, be with us in the Sacrament of
the Eucharist.
Holy Spirit, help us grow as members of the
Body of Christ.

Reader: Listen to God's message to us:
(Read John 6:32–40.)
The word of the Lord.

All: **Thanks be to God.**

Leader: Let us ask God's blessing on our journey together.

All: **Holy Trinity, lead us to the table of the Eucharist.**
Teach us to love one another as you love us.
Help us be living signs of your presence in
our midst,
and lead us to the fullness of your kingdom.
We pray in the words that Jesus taught us.
(Pray the Lord's Prayer.)

Leader: May the Lord be with us, now and always.

All: **Amen!**

CHAPTER 1

BELONGING

Dear God—Father, Son, and Holy Spirit—
you call us to new life.
Help us grow as members of the Church.
Amen!

Everyone needs to belong. When you belong,
you share time and love with others. You help
people, and they help you.

When did you become a member of
your family?

You belong to the Catholic Church, too. You became a member of the Church when you were baptized.

Belonging to the Church means belonging to God, forever. When you were baptized, you became a follower of Jesus Christ. You became a **Christian**.

In the Name of Jesus Christ

I remember that morning. I was in Jerusalem with my family for the Jewish feast of **Pentecost**. We saw a great crowd gathered. A man named Peter was speaking.

"Friends!" Peter said in a loud voice. You know that Jesus was a great teacher sent by God. Jesus died on a cross, but that was not the end of the story!"

"God set Jesus free from death," Peter continued. "Jesus rose from the tomb, and now he is with his Father in heaven. This very day he sent the **Holy Spirit** to us as he had promised. That promise is not just for us, his friends. It is for you and your children, too!"

"What must we do?" my father called out.

"Turn to God, my friend," Peter answered. "Be baptized in the name of Jesus Christ. Then you will receive God's Holy Spirit, too."

That morning I was baptized with my whole family. Now we all belong to the family of Jesus Christ.

—*based on Acts 2*

Baptism and Confirmation

The Catholic Church welcomes new members through Baptism, Confirmation, and Eucharist. These sacraments are called **Sacraments of Initiation**, or "belonging."

We celebrate Baptism with water and holy words. All living things need water to stay alive. We need the water of Baptism to have new life forever with God.

The words of Baptism tell us that we belong to God. "I baptize you in the name of the Father, and of the Son, and of the Holy Spirit."

We celebrate Confirmation by being **anointed** with holy oil and by the laying on of hands. Oil is used to make the body strong. Confirmation helps us grow strong in our faith. We reach out to others who need God's love.

The words of Confirmation tell us that we have been given the Holy Spirit in a special way. "Be sealed with the Gift of the Holy Spirit."

We Ask

Why is Baptism the first sacrament?

Baptism makes us members of the Church and joins us to Jesus. In Baptism we first share in the **Paschal mystery** of Jesus' death and **resurrection**. All the other sacraments build on the grace of Baptism. (Catechism, #1213–1214)

I Am Signed with the Cross

On the cross, write or draw one way you can show that you belong to Jesus Christ and the Church.

The Grace of Baptism

Every time we recall our Baptism, we
remember Jesus' life, death, and resurrection.

Through Baptism and Confirmation,
make us faithful followers of Jesus Christ.

   Lord, hear our prayer.

Lead us by a holy life
to the joys of God's kingdom.

   Lord, hear our prayer.

Make the lives of our families and godparents
signs of faith for us to follow.

   Lord, hear our prayer.

Keep our families always in God's love.

   Lord, hear our prayer.

Renew the grace of Baptism in each of us.

   Lord, hear our prayer.

—based on the Rite of Baptism

CHAPTER 2
INVITED TO THE TABLE

Dear God—Father, Son, and Holy Spirit—
you have called us to the table of the Eucharist.
Help us live as members of the Body of Christ.
Amen!

What if you went to a family party and there
was no place for you at the dinner table? You
would probably feel left out. Sharing a meal is
a big part of any celebration. When you are
invited to sit at
the table, you
really feel that
you belong.

What do you
like best about
sharing meals?

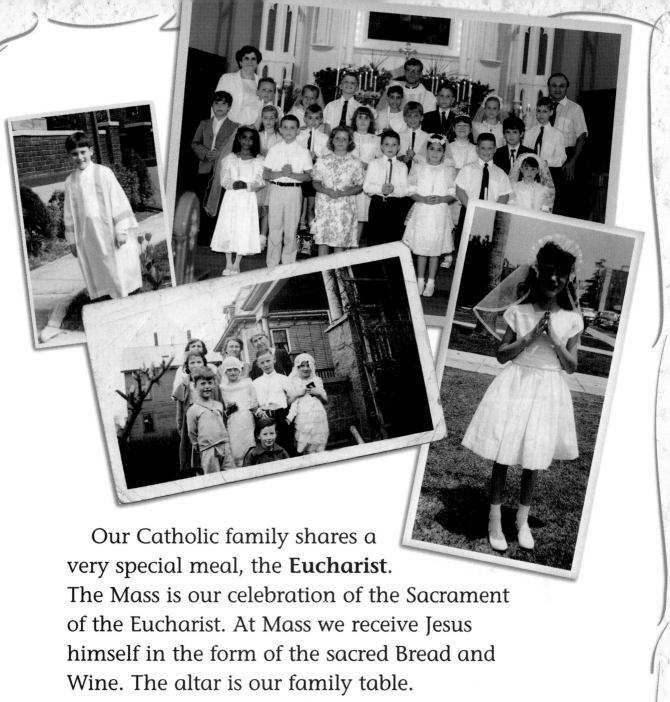

Our Catholic family shares a very special meal, the **Eucharist**. The Mass is our celebration of the Sacrament of the Eucharist. At Mass we receive Jesus himself in the form of the sacred Bread and Wine. The altar is our family table.

You have celebrated the Eucharist before by coming to Mass with your family and your class. But now you are getting ready to share completely in our holy meal. You are invited to come to the table and receive Jesus in **Holy Communion**.

The Vine and the Branches

On the night before he died, Jesus went with his friends to a garden to pray. Jesus' friends were sad. They thought they would never see Jesus again. They wanted to stay close to him.

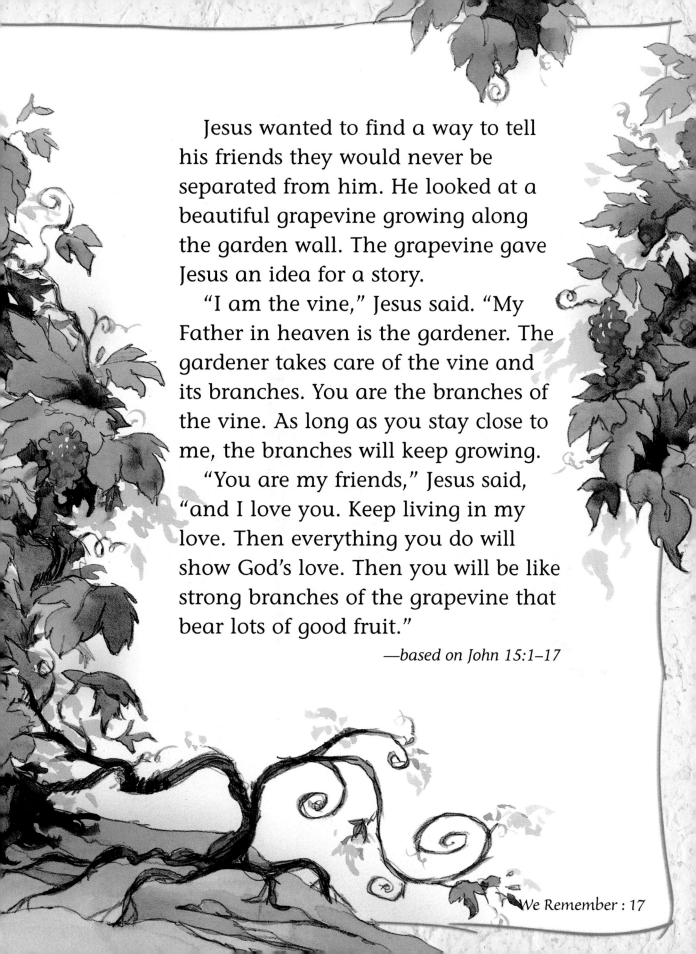

Jesus wanted to find a way to tell his friends they would never be separated from him. He looked at a beautiful grapevine growing along the garden wall. The grapevine gave Jesus an idea for a story.

"I am the vine," Jesus said. "My Father in heaven is the gardener. The gardener takes care of the vine and its branches. You are the branches of the vine. As long as you stay close to me, the branches will keep growing.

"You are my friends," Jesus said, "and I love you. Keep living in my love. Then everything you do will show God's love. Then you will be like strong branches of the grapevine that bear lots of good fruit."

—based on John 15:1–17

First Communion

We want to be joined closely to Jesus like the branches of the grapevine. So we celebrate the Sacraments of Initiation. We are baptized. We are sealed with the Holy Spirit in Confirmation. We receive Jesus in Holy Communion for the first time.

The Sacraments of Initiation join us together with Jesus and with all his followers. We are the **Body of Christ**.

People of all ages celebrate the Sacraments of Initiation to become full members of the Church. Some Catholics celebrate all three sacraments at the same time. Other Catholics are baptized as babies. Then around the age of seven they celebrate First Reconciliation and First Communion. They are confirmed some time later.

We Ask

How often should we receive Communion?

Baptism and Confirmation are once-in-a-lifetime celebrations. They mark us as God's own forever. But once we have received First Communion, we are encouraged to come to the table again and again throughout our lives. Each time we celebrate the Eucharist at Mass, we should receive Jesus in Communion if we are free of serious sin. *(Catechism, #1388)*

My Answer to Jesus

Jesus invites you to grow closer to him by receiving your First Communion. Finish the sentence in your own words. Sign your name.

Dear Jesus,
Thank you for inviting me to the table of the Eucharist. I want to receive Communion because

_____

_____

_____

_____

Love,

_____

Together to One Table

We thank God for the gift of the Eucharist.

God our Father,
Jesus brought us the good news.
He showed us the way of love.
He brings us together to one table
and asks us to do what he did.
Glory to God in the highest!
Father in heaven,
you have called us to receive
the Body and Blood of Christ at this table
and be filled with the joy of the Holy Spirit.
Through this holy meal, give us the strength
to please you more and more.
Glory to God in the highest!

—based on Eucharistic Prayer III for Children

CHAPTER 3
GATHERING TO CELEBRATE

Dear God—Father, Son, and Holy Spirit—
we come together as a family at Mass.
Welcome us as we welcome one another.
Amen!

It's no fun to celebrate alone. Good times are better when you share them with others. Family members, friends, and neighbors are part of your **community**, the group of people with whom you share special times.

What are some things you like to do when you get together with family members and friends?

We celebrate the Eucharist with a community, too. We come together for Mass with members of our Church family, the **parish**.

Gathering for Mass is like gathering for other celebrations. We greet one another. We share our joy in singing. We remember God's mercy and forgiveness.

Like Family to One Another

The first Christians made the Eucharist the center of their lives. Every week they went to the Temple to pray, just as they always had. Then they gathered in one home or another to remember Jesus.

Before sharing the Lord's Body and Blood, the people remembered with joy their Baptism and the coming of the Holy Spirit. They sang songs of praise to God.

The Christians were like family to one another. Everyone was welcome. Everyone shared. Rich people shared what they had with those who were poor. People who had no money shared their prayers and their talents, helping one another.

These first followers of Jesus amazed all who saw them. "Look!" the people said. "See how these Christians love one another!"

—*based on Acts 2:42–47*

The Mass Begins

From the very beginning, it's easy to see that the Mass is a celebration. We begin with a song and a parade. The song is a **hymn**, or holy song. The parade is a **procession** of ministers who will help us celebrate.

The prayers and actions of the beginning of the Mass are called the **Introductory Rites**. They help us turn our hearts and minds to the great celebration of the Eucharist.

Jesus is really present in every part of the Mass. He is most truly with us in Communion, but he is also with us in the priest who **presides** over, or leads, our celebration. He is present in the other ministers. He is present in all of us, the **assembly**.

At Mass we gather to celebrate the same Paschal mystery we celebrate in Baptism. We bless ourselves with water from the baptismal font or holy water font when we come into the church. The Mass begins with the Sign of the Cross, the same words with which we were baptized. "In the name of the Father, and of the Son, and of the Holy Spirit. Amen!"

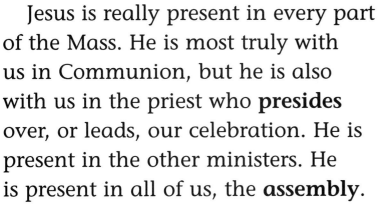

Why do we celebrate the Eucharist every week?

Gathering for Mass every week is how we show that we belong to the Body of Christ. We have a **duty** to participate in the Mass once a week, on Sunday or on Saturday evening, and on holy days. The more we celebrate, the closer we come to Jesus and to one another.
(Catechism, #2180–2182)

I Come to Celebrate

In the space below, draw or glue pictures of people who will gather at Mass to celebrate with you on the day you receive First Communion.

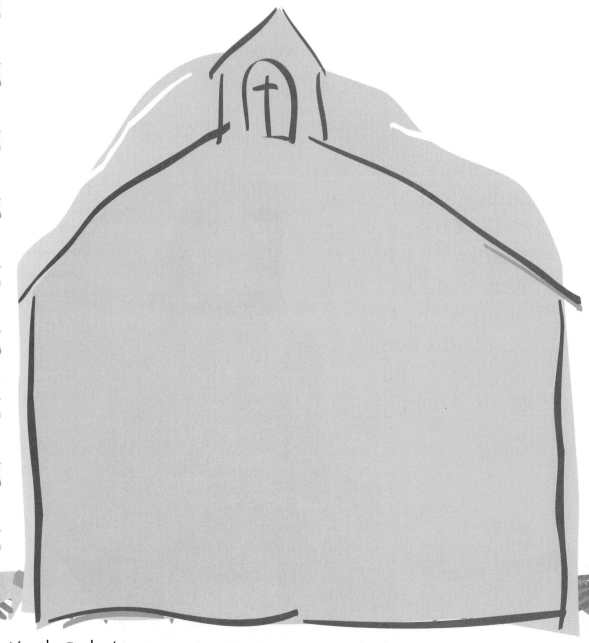

Lord, Have Mercy

In the Penitential Rite at Mass, we recall God's mercy and forgiveness as we celebrate together.

Coming together as God's family,
with confidence let us ask the Father's
    forgiveness,
for he is full of gentleness and kindness.
Lord Jesus, you raise us to new life.
   Lord, have mercy.
Lord Jesus, you forgive us our sins.
   Lord, have mercy.
Lord Jesus, you feed us with your Body
   and Blood.
   Lord, have mercy.

—*based on the Order of the Mass*

CHAPTER 4
FEASTING ON GOD'S WORD

Dear God—Father, Son, and Holy Spirit—
your word is good news to us.
Help us hear your word and live by it.
Amen!

Some stories are so good you want to hear
them over and over. Good stories are like
good news. They make you laugh or give you
hope. A good story can be like a feast of good
food, shared with people you love.

What is one of your favorite stories?

Our Catholic family shares wonderful stories, too. At Mass we hear the good news of God's love in the words of the **Scriptures**. When we listen, it is as though God is speaking right to us. The feast of God's word is part of the holy meal of the Eucharist.

Jesus, the Good Shepherd

Jesus knew that people needed to hear the good news of God's love. So one day Jesus compared himself to a shepherd, a person who cares for a flock of sheep. In Jesus' day almost everyone had seen shepherds at work in the fields.

"I am the good shepherd," Jesus told the people. "Just as a shepherd cares for all the sheep, so I care for you. I know you by name, just as a shepherd knows his sheep."

Jesus continued. "You have seen how a shepherd lies down in front of the sheep gate at night, to stay on guard. When the shepherd is there, the sheep are safe. Even if a wolf comes, the good shepherd will not run away. The good shepherd would rather die than see one of the sheep hurt. In the same way, I will give up my life so that you will be saved."

Not everyone in the crowd understood
Jesus' story, but some people did. The
people who listened and understood
were happy. They knew God loved them
very much.

—based on John 10:1–18

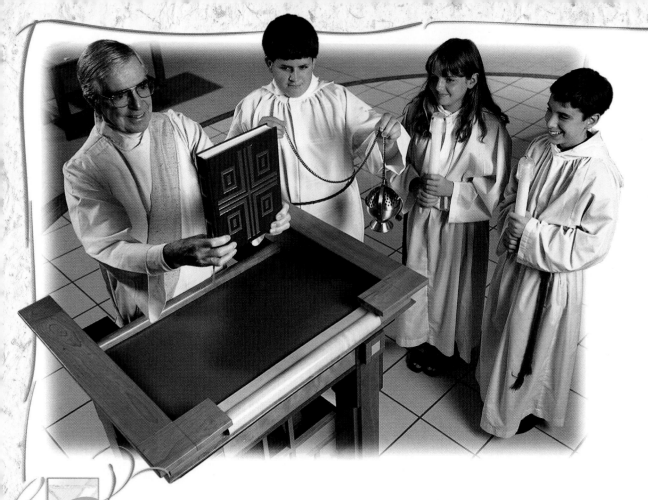

Sharing the Word

We share God's word in the part of the Mass called the **Liturgy of the Word**. At Sunday Mass we hear three readings from the Bible. Between the first two readings, we sing or pray a **psalm** as our response, or answer, to God's word.

The readings tell us the good news of God's love. In fact, the third reading is called the **gospel**, which means "good news." This reading is from the part of the Bible that tells about Jesus' life and teachings. We greet the gospel reading with a song or shout of joy, **"Alleluia!"**

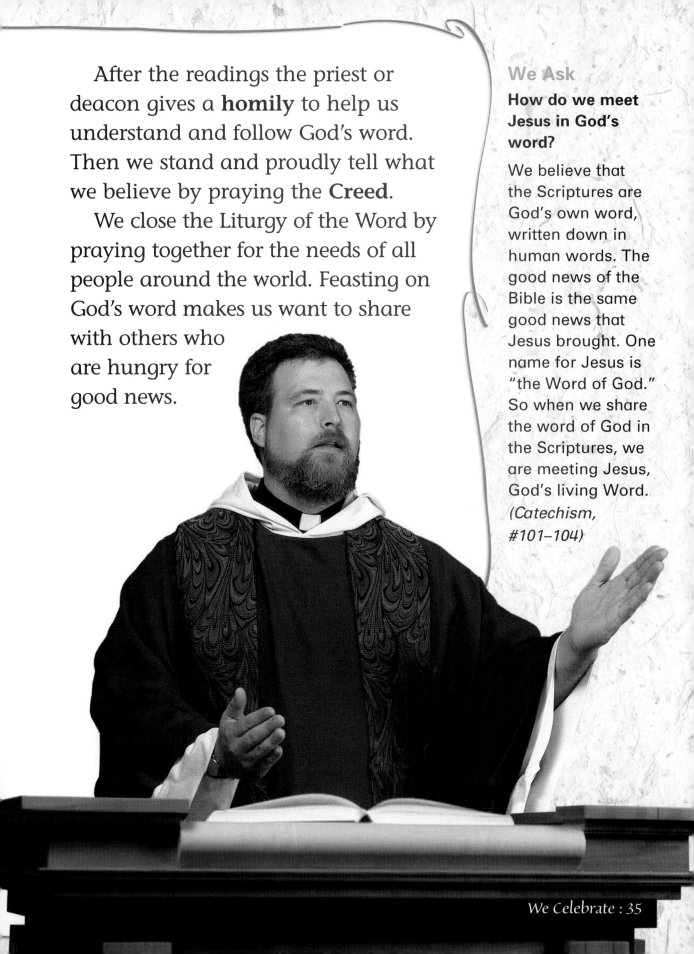

After the readings the priest or deacon gives a **homily** to help us understand and follow God's word. Then we stand and proudly tell what we believe by praying the **Creed**.

We close the Liturgy of the Word by praying together for the needs of all people around the world. Feasting on God's word makes us want to share with others who are hungry for good news.

How do we meet Jesus in God's word?

We believe that the Scriptures are God's own word, written down in human words. The good news of the Bible is the same good news that Jesus brought. One name for Jesus is "the Word of God." So when we share the word of God in the Scriptures, we are meeting Jesus, God's living Word. *(Catechism, #101–104)*

I Hear Good News

In the space below, draw or write about one of your favorite Bible stories.

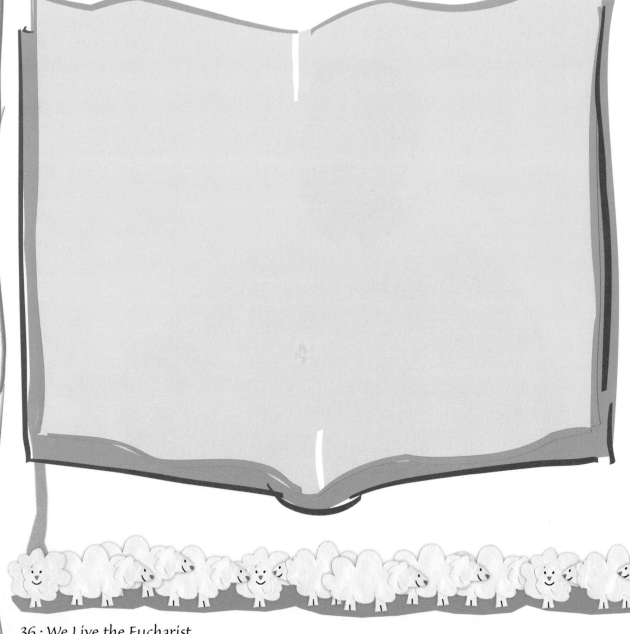

You Treat Us to a Feast

We pray to the Lord, our good shepherd, in the words of a psalm.

You, Lord, are our shepherd.
We will never be in need.
You let us rest in fields of green grass.
You lead us to streams of peaceful water.
    You, Lord, are our shepherd.
You treat us to a feast.
You honor us as your guests,
and you fill our cup until it overflows.
    You, Lord, are our shepherd.
Your kindness and love will always be with us,
each day of our lives,
and we will live forever in your house, Lord.
    You, Lord, are our shepherd.

—based on Psalm 23

CHAPTER 5
OFFERING OUR GIFTS

Dear God—Father, Son, and Holy Spirit—
you give us every good thing.
Help us share our gifts with others.
Amen!

When people gather for a special meal, they
sometimes bring gifts of food.

What special foods does your family share?
What kind of food would you bring to a
special meal?

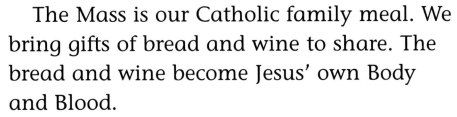

The Mass is our Catholic family meal. We bring gifts of bread and wine to share. The bread and wine become Jesus' own Body and Blood.

We share other things at Mass, too. We offer the gift of ourselves to God and to one another. We offer gifts of money to support the work of the parish and to help those who are in need.

The Wonderful Picnic

"Does anyone have any food to share?" I heard the man named Philip ask. Thousands of people were sitting on the grass listening to Jesus teach. All the people shook their heads. No one had thought to bring food.

I took a deep breath. "Sir!" I called out. I have five loaves of bread and a couple of fish."

The people around me laughed. Philip looked angry. "That's not enough food to feed even five people, never mind five thousand!" he said.

But I was looking at Jesus. He was smiling. He motioned for me to come forward. Jesus looked into my eyes and thanked me. He took the basket of food I held out to him.

Jesus took the bread in his hands and prayed the meal blessing. "Philip," he said. "You and the others pass this food to the people. Make sure everyone has enough to eat."

Something wonderful happened that day. From my five loaves and two fish, more than five thousand people had the best picnic ever. When the meal was finished, there were twelve baskets of leftovers!

"Thank you for sharing," Jesus said to me. And even Philip smiled.

—*based on John 6:5–13*

Our Offering to God

The second part of the Mass, following the Liturgy of the Word, is called the **Liturgy of the Eucharist**. During this part of the Mass, we offer our gifts and prayers to God the Father. Our greatest offering is Jesus, who offers himself to the Father through the Holy Spirit. In the form of the sacred Bread and Wine, Jesus offers himself to us in Holy Communion.

At the **presentation of gifts**, members of the assembly bring the bread and wine to the priest. These gifts are placed on the **altar**, the table of offering. The priest blesses the bread and wine.

Along with the gifts of bread and wine, we offer gifts of money. This offering is called a **collection**. The money will help the parish community do its work and take care of those in need.

The money offering is also a sign that we offer ourselves to God. We are willing to share our time and our talents, as well as our treasure, with one another.

We Ask

Why do we call the Mass a sacrifice?

In the Eucharist we remember and celebrate Jesus' **sacrifice** for us on the cross. Jesus offered his life to his Father to save us from the power of sin and everlasting death. At every Mass Jesus' sacrifice is made present. We offer ourselves and our gifts, too.
The whole Church joins with Jesus in the sacrifice of the Mass.
(Catechism, #1366–1368)

I Share My Gifts

In the space below, write about or draw two gifts you can offer to God and share with the Christian community.

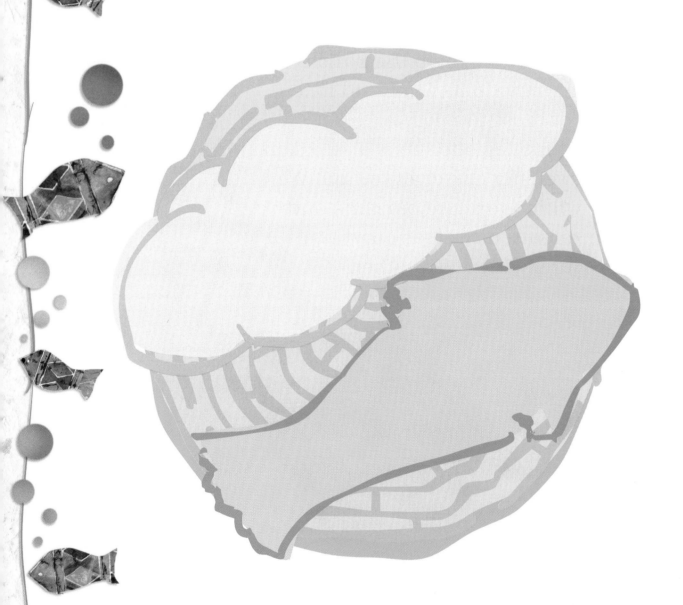

Through Your Goodness

We ask God to bless our gifts of bread and wine, just as we ask God to bless our food before every meal.

Blessed are you, Lord, God of all creation.
Through your goodness
we have this bread to offer,
which earth has given
and human hands have made.
It will become for us the bread of life.
Blessed be God forever!

Blessed are you, Lord, God of all creation.
Through your goodness
we have this wine to offer,
fruit of the vine and work of human hands.
It will become our spiritual drink.
Blessed be God forever!

—from the Order of the Mass

CHAPTER 6

REMEMBERING AND GIVING THANKS

Dear God—Father, Son, and Holy Spirit—
we remember how much you care for us.
We thank you for your love that saves us.
Amen!

Every year families in our country
share a special holiday. We remember
the good things God has done for us.
We share a meal. We call this holiday
Thanksgiving because we give thanks
to God for our families and our country.
What things do you thank God for?

We give thanks to God at Mass, too. In fact, the word **Eucharist** means "thanksgiving." In the Eucharist we remember that God our Father sent Jesus to save us. We give thanks and lift our hearts to God in prayer. We get ready to share the holy meal of the Eucharist.

Jesus Gives Thanks

On the night before he died, Jesus shared a special meal with his friends. They gathered to celebrate the **Passover**, a great Jewish holiday of thanksgiving.

Long ago God led the people of Israel out of the land of Egypt, where they had been slaves. He saved the people and set them free. Every year at the Passover meal, Jewish people remember God's saving love.

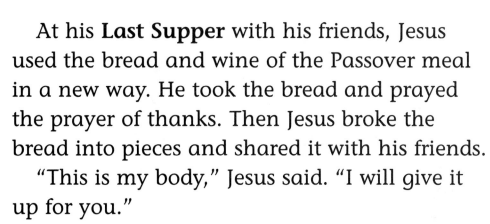

At his **Last Supper** with his friends, Jesus used the bread and wine of the Passover meal in a new way. He took the bread and prayed the prayer of thanks. Then Jesus broke the bread into pieces and shared it with his friends.

"This is my body," Jesus said. "I will give it up for you."

Then Jesus took a cup of wine. Again he thanked God, his Father. He passed the cup to his friends.

"Drink this," Jesus said. "This is the cup of my blood. This blood will be poured out to save you and set you free."

Jesus looked at his friends with love. "Whenever you do this," he said, "remember me!"

—*based on Matthew 26:17–19, 26–28*

Our Great Thanksgiving Prayer

At Mass we do what Jesus did at his Last Supper with his friends. And we do remember him.

The most important prayer of the Mass is called the **Eucharistic Prayer**. It is our prayer of thanksgiving to God our Father.

During the Eucharistic Prayer the priest repeats the words and actions of Jesus at the Last Supper. "This is my body," he says. "This is the cup of my blood."

Through the words of Christ and the power of the Holy Spirit, the bread and wine truly become Jesus' Body and Blood. He is really with us in our thanksgiving meal, the Eucharist.

"Amen!" we pray. "Yes, we do believe!"

We Ask

Do the bread and wine really become Jesus' Body and Blood?

Yes. We believe that when the bread and wine are **consecrated** at Mass, they are no longer bread and wine. Jesus is truly and really present. We don't fully understand how this great **mystery** of our faith happens. We believe and trust that Jesus is with us because he promised he would be.
(Catechism, #1333)

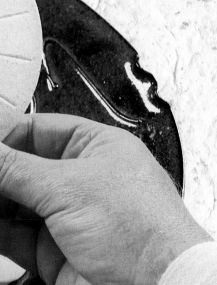

I Remember, I Give Thanks

Finish the prayers by writing or drawing in each box.

Dear God, I remember you love me when I . . .

Dear God, I give thanks to you for . . .

We Give Thanks

God gives us so much. We can
celebrate Thanksgiving every day.

God our Father,
you have brought us here together
so that we can give you thanks and praise
for all the wonderful things you have done.
We know that you are good.
You love us and do great things for us!
We thank you for all that is beautiful
   in the world
and for the happiness you have given us.
We know that you are good.
You love us and do great things for us!
We praise you for the earth
and for the people who live on it
and for our life, which comes from you.
We know that you are good.
You love us and do great things for us!

—*based on Eucharistic Prayer I for Children*

CHAPTER 7
SHARING THE BREAD OF LIFE

Dear God—Father, Son, and Holy Spirit—
you feed us at the table of the Eucharist.
Keep us close to you forever.
Amen!

Sharing a meal brings people closer together.
A special party meal, sometimes called a
banquet or a feast, is a time to celebrate.
Family members and friends grow in love.

Have you ever shared in a banquet? Who
was there? How did you feel?

The Eucharist is our banquet. God invites us to the table to share Jesus' own Body and Blood in Communion. Before we come to the table, we pray the **Lord's Prayer**. This is the family prayer of the followers of Jesus. "Give us this day our daily bread," we pray, "and forgive us our trespasses."

To show that we are willing to forgive one another and make up, we exchange a **sign of peace**. Then the priest breaks the large Host as Jesus broke the sacred Bread at his Last Supper. We welcome Jesus as the **Lamb of God**, who takes away our sins and brings us peace.

The Bread That Gives Life

After Jesus had fed the crowd with only five loaves of bread and a few fish, people wanted him to perform more **miracles**. "You are like Moses," the people said. "When the people of Israel were hungry in the desert, Moses gave them **manna**, bread from heaven."

"You are not remembering the whole story," Jesus told them. "It was not Moses who gave food to the people. It was God, our Father in heaven. God gives people the real bread from heaven."

"Lord, give us this bread always!" the people begged.

"I myself am the bread that gives life," Jesus answered. "My Father sent me to bring you life that lasts forever. No one who comes to me will ever be hungry. No one who believes in me will ever be thirsty."

Jesus continued. "I am the bread from heaven. The people who ate manna in the desert eventually died, as all humans die. But if you share my own flesh and blood, you will live forever with God."

"What is he talking about?" some people asked. But others remembered how they felt when Jesus fed them with bread and fish. They believed what he said.

—*based on John 6:30–58*

Holy Communion

When the time comes for Communion, the priest invites us to the table. "This is the Lamb of God, who takes away the sin of the world," he says, holding up the large Host. "Happy are we who are called to his supper!"

To receive Communion, we come forward in a procession. We wait our turn respectfully. We hold our hands up, cupping them with one hand on top of the other. The priest or **Eucharistic minister** places the Host in our hands and says, "The Body of Christ." We answer, "Amen!"

Then we step aside and eat the sacred Bread.

On many Sundays we may also receive Communion from the cup. After swallowing the Host, we go to the deacon or Eucharistic minister who is holding the cup of consecrated Wine. The minister says, "The Blood of Christ." We answer, "Amen!" When we are offered the cup, we take a small sip.

Jesus is truly present in both forms of the Eucharist.

After receiving Communion, we return to our places. There may be a Communion song or a time of silent prayer.

We Ask

Who can receive Communion?

Baptized Catholics who have celebrated First Communion may receive Communion at Mass. A person who has committed mortal sin must receive **absolution** in the **Sacrament of Reconciliation** before receiving Communion. *(Catechism, #1384–1389)*

My First Communion

In the frame, draw or glue a picture of your First Communion. On the line, write the date of your First Communion.

_____

Bread from Heaven

We thank God for the gift of the Eucharist.

Father,
you increase our faith and hope,
you deepen our love in Holy Communion.
Help us live by your words
and seek Christ, our Bread of Life,
who is Lord for ever and ever.

Amen!

Lord, you feed us with bread from heaven.
Fill us with your Spirit,
and make us one in peace and love.

Amen!

May we who share at this table
be filled with your love
and prepared for the joy of your kingdom,
where Jesus is Lord for ever and ever.

Amen!

—*based on Prayers after Communion*

Chapter 8
GOING FORTH TO LOVE AND SERVE

Dear God—Father, Son, and Holy Spirit—thank you for coming to us in the Eucharist. Send us out into the world to share your love. Amen!

Have you ever been sent to tell someone something or to do a special job?

Being sent means that you are trusted. You are responsible. Someone is counting on you. Without you the message will not be shared. The job will not get done.

At the end of the Mass, each of us is sent to carry the message of God's love. We are sent to help carry out the work of Jesus in the world. Even the word **Mass** comes from a word that means "to be sent on a **mission**."

No one is too young or too old to be trusted with this mission. The Eucharist gives us what we need to bring good news to others. Receiving Jesus in Holy Communion strengthens us to love and serve. We go out with God's blessing.

In the Breaking of the Bread

It was the third day after Jesus died on the cross. Cleopas and I were walking home from Jerusalem to our town, Emmaus. We were sad.

Then another traveler joined us. We did not know who he was. He asked us why we were so sad.

Cleopas and I told the traveler all about Jesus. We talked about what a great teacher he was and how he fed us with Bread from heaven. We thought he was the **Messiah** sent by God to save us. But now he was dead.

The traveler shook his head. "Foolish people!" he said. "Don't you know that the Scriptures say the Messiah will give up his life for you?" And he explained God's word to us as we walked along.

We reached home as the sun was setting. "Stay and eat with us," Cleopas invited the traveler. "It's nearly night."

As we sat at the table, the traveler took the bread. He blessed it and broke it. And as he gave it to us, we suddenly understood. The traveler was Jesus! God the Father had raised him from death!

In the blink of an eye, Jesus was gone. We ran all the way back to Jerusalem. We burst into the room where Jesus' mother and his friends had gathered.

"Jesus is alive!" Peter said as he greeted us joyfully.

"We know!" I said. "He walked with us on the road. He shared God's word with us. And we recognized him in the breaking of the Bread."

—*based on Luke 24:13–35*

We Are Sent

Like Cleopas and his friend, we meet Jesus in the breaking of the sacred Bread. In the Eucharist Jesus walks with us. He shares God's word with us. Jesus offers his life to the Father in the power of the Holy Spirit. He comes to us in Communion.

And like those friends of Jesus, we want to share the joyful good news that Jesus is alive. At the end of the Mass, we are sent out to serve others. "Go in peace to love and serve the Lord," the priest or deacon says. "Thanks be to God!" we answer.

When we leave the church after Mass, we are different from when we came in. The Eucharist changes us. It brings us closer to God and to one another. The Eucharist takes away our less serious sins. It helps us make peace with everyone.

In the Eucharist we become one body, just as many grains of wheat make one loaf of bread. So when we go out into the world, we recognize Jesus in everyone. We love and serve Jesus when we love and serve one another.

We Ask

How is the Eucharist a sign of God's kingdom?

Jesus came to announce God's kingdom of justice, love, and peace. That kingdom is both here in our midst and yet to come in fullness. In the Eucharist we receive a taste of the heavenly banquet we will share with all faithful people in the fullness of God's kingdom. Strengthened by the Eucharist, we work to bring justice, love, and peace to everyone. *(Catechism, #1402–1405)*

I Love and Serve

Draw or write three things you will do to share God's love with others.

One in Christ

We pray that God will help us live always as members of the Body of Christ.

God our Father,
you have called us to share
the one bread and one cup
and so become one in Christ.
Help us live in him
that we may bear fruit,
rejoicing that he has redeemed the world.
We ask this through Christ our Lord.
   Amen!

May almighty God bless us,
the Father, the Son, and the Holy Spirit.
   Amen!

—*from the Sacramentary*

Catholic Prayers

The Sign of the Cross

In the name of the Father,
and of the Son,
and of the Holy Spirit.
Amen.

The Lord's Prayer

Our Father, who art in heaven,
hallowed be thy name;
thy kingdom come;
thy will be done on earth as it is in heaven.
Give us this day our daily bread;
and forgive us our trespasses
as we forgive those who trespass against us;
and lead us not into temptation,
but deliver us from evil.
Amen.

Hail Mary

Hail, Mary, full of grace,
the Lord is with you!
Blessed are you among women,
and blessed is the fruit of your womb, Jesus.
Holy Mary, Mother of God,
pray for us sinners,
now and at the hour of our death.
Amen.

Glory to the Father (Doxology)

Glory to the Father,
and to the Son,
and to the Holy Spirit,
as it was in the beginning,
is now, and will be for ever.
Amen.

Blessing Before First Communion

May the Lord Jesus touch your ears to receive his word,
and your mouth to proclaim his faith.
May you come with joy to his supper
to the praise and glory of God.
Amen.

Prayer Before Communion

How holy is this feast
in which Christ is our food:
his passion is recalled,
grace fills our hearts,
and we receive a pledge of the glory to come.

—based on a prayer of Thomas Aquinas

Thanksgiving After Communion

Lord our God,
we honor the memory of Saint Pius X
and all your saints
by sharing the bread of heaven.
May it strengthen our faith
and unite us in your love.
We ask this in the name of Jesus the Lord.
Amen.

The Life of Jesus

Here are some of the important events in Jesus' life as they are described in the Gospels.

The Annunciation

God sent the Angel Gabriel to tell Mary she was going to be the mother of Jesus, God's own Son.

The Nativity

Jesus was born in Bethlehem in a shelter for animals. Angels told shepherds the good news that the Savior was born.

The Presentation

At the Temple in Jerusalem, Mary and Joseph offered a sacrifice of thanksgiving for Jesus' birth. Simeon and Anna, two prophets, recognized Jesus as the Messiah.

The Epiphany

Wise teachers from faraway lands came to worship Jesus.

The Escape to Egypt

An angry king threatened to kill Jesus. Joseph, his foster father, was warned in a dream to take Mary and Jesus to Egypt.

The Young Jesus in the Temple

On a trip to Jerusalem for the Passover, Jesus became separated from Mary and Joseph. They looked for him and found him in the Temple, talking about God's word with wise teachers.

Jesus' Baptism by John

When Jesus was about thirty years old, he began his public life of teaching. He was baptized in the Jordan River by his cousin John, a prophet.

The Temptation in the Desert

After his baptism Jesus went alone to the desert to pray and fast. He was tempted by Satan, but he remained true to God, his Father.

Jesus Calls the Apostles

Jesus gathered a group of special friends and helpers called the apostles. Other men and women also followed Jesus and helped him in his work.

Jesus Teaches

Jesus taught crowds of people about God's love. He told stories called parables.

Jesus Heals

In the name of God, his Father, Jesus healed people who were sick or troubled. He forgave sins.

Jesus Shows God's Love

Jesus worked miracles, or powerful signs of God's love. He changed water into wine at a marriage feast. He fed thousands of people with only a little food. He brought people who were dead back to life.

Jesus Enters Jerusalem

After about three years of teaching, Jesus entered Jerusalem for the Passover. He knew he faced death because certain leaders were angry with him. Some people, waving palm branches, welcomed Jesus as a king as he rode into the city.

The Last Supper

On the night before he died, Jesus celebrated the Passover meal with his friends. He washed their feet as a sign that they should serve others. He shared himself with them in the first Eucharist.

In the Garden

After supper Jesus went to a garden with his friends to pray. One of his friends betrayed him by turning Jesus over to the leaders who wanted to kill him. Jesus was arrested and taken to jail.

The Trial

Jesus was accused of acting against the law. He was whipped and beaten. The leaders sentenced Jesus to death.

The Crucifixion

Jesus was executed by being nailed to a cross. While he hung on the cross,

he forgave those who had sentenced him. Then Jesus died.

The Burial

Jesus' body was taken to a tomb. The tomb was sealed with a large stone.

The Resurrection

On the third day after Jesus' death, God the Father raised him to new life. When Jesus' friends visited his tomb, they found the stone removed and the tomb empty. Later Jesus himself appeared to them in glory.

The Ascension

Forty days after the resurrection, Jesus returned to his Father in heaven. Jesus promised to send the Holy Spirit to teach and guide the Church.

Holy Communion

Receiving Holy Communion

Catholics follow these rules and practices to show respect for the Eucharist:

- Only baptized Catholics may receive Communion.

- To receive Holy Communion, we must be free from mortal sin. We must be sorry for any venial sins committed since the last time we celebrated the Sacrament of Reconciliation. When we have contrition, receiving Holy Communion frees us from venial sin.

- To honor the Lord, we fast for one hour before receiving Communion. We go without food or drink, except water or medicine.

- Catholics are required to receive Holy Communion at least once a year, if possible during Easter time. But we are encouraged to receive Communion every time we participate in the Mass.

- Catholics are permitted to receive Communion at a second Mass on the same day.

How to Receive Communion

When we receive Jesus in Holy Communion, we welcome him with our whole bodies, minds, and spirits.

Here are steps to follow when you receive Communion:

- Fold your hands, and join in singing the Communion hymn as you walk to the altar.

- When it is your turn, you can receive the consecrated Host in your hand or on your tongue. To receive it in your hand, hold your hands out with the palms up. Place one hand underneath the other, and cup your hands slightly. To receive the Host on your tongue, fold your hands, and open your mouth, putting your tongue out.

- The priest or Eucharistic minister says, "The Body of Christ," and you answer, "Amen." The priest or minister places the Host in your hand or on your tongue.

- Step aside and stop. If you have received the Host in your hand, carefully take it from your palm, and put it in your mouth. Chew and swallow the Host.

- You may also be offered Communion from the cup. After swallowing the Host, walk to where the cup is offered. The deacon or Eucharistic minister says, "The Blood of Christ." You answer, "Amen."

- Take the cup from the priest, deacon, or minister. Take a small sip, and carefully hand the cup back.

- Quietly return to your place. Pray a prayer of thanksgiving.

Illustrated Glossary of the Mass

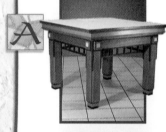

altar
(AWL•ter): The table of the Eucharist. At the altar the sacrifice of the Mass is offered to God.

ambo
(AM•boh): The lectern, or reading stand, from which the Scriptures are proclaimed. The ambo is sometimes called "the table of the word."

assembly
(uh•SEM•blee): The community gathered to celebrate the Eucharist or another sacramental liturgy.

baptismal font
(bap•TIZ•muhl FAHNT): The bowl-shaped container or pool of water used for Baptism. The word *font* means "fountain."

Book of the Gospels
(BUK uhv thuh GAHS•puhlz): A decorated book containing the readings from the four Gospels used during the Liturgy of the Word.

cantor

(KAN•ter): The minister who leads the singing at Mass and during other Church celebrations.

chalice

(CHA•luhs): The special cup used at Mass to hold the wine that becomes the Blood of Christ.

ciborium

(suh•BOHR•ee•uhm): A container for hosts. A ciborium may hold the smaller consecrated Hosts used for Communion. A covered ciborium also holds the Blessed Sacrament in the tabernacle.

cruets

(KROO•uhts): Small pitchers or containers for the water and wine used at Mass. Many parishes use larger pitchers to hold the wine, especially if people will be receiving Communion from the cup.

deacon

(DEE•kuhn): A man who is ordained to serve the Church by baptizing, proclaiming the gospel, preaching, assisting the priest at Mass, witnessing marriages, and doing works of charity.

E

Eucharist

(YOO•kuh•ruhst): The sacrament of Jesus' presence under the form of sacred Bread and Wine. We receive Jesus' own Body and Blood as Holy Communion during the Eucharistic celebration, the Mass. The word *Eucharist* means "thanksgiving."

H

host

(HOHST): A round piece of unleavened bread used at Mass. When the host is consecrated, it becomes the Body and Blood of Christ. We receive the consecrated Host in Holy Communion.

I

incense

(IN•sents): Oils and spices that are burned to make sweet-smelling smoke. At Mass and in other liturgical celebrations, incense is sometimes used to show honor for holy things and as a sign of our prayers rising to God.

L

Lectionary

(LEK•shuh•nair•ee): The book of the Scripture readings used at Mass.

lector

(LEK•ter): A minister who proclaims God's word at Mass or during other liturgical celebrations. The word *lector* means "reader."

offering

(AW•fuh•ring): The gifts we give at Mass. Members of the assembly bring our offering of bread and wine to the altar. We also give an offering of money, called a *collection*, to support the work of the Church.

paten

(PA•tuhn): The plate or dish used at Mass to hold the bread that will become the Body and Blood of Christ.

priest

(PREEST): A man who is ordained to serve God and the Church by celebrating the sacraments, preaching, and presiding at Mass.

Sacramentary

(sa•kruh•MEN•tair•ee): The book of prayers used by the priest at Mass. Another name for this book is the **missal** (MIH•suhl). Members of the assembly may use booklets called **missalettes** (mih•suh•LETS) to follow the readings and join in the responses and prayers.

sanctuary

(SANGK•chuh•wair•ee): The part of the church where the altar and the ambo are located. The word *sanctuary* means "holy place."

server

(SER•ver): A minister, usually a young person, who helps the priest and deacon at Mass. An older person who carries out this ministry is known as an **acolyte** (A•koh•lyt).

tabernacle

(TA•buhr•na•kuhl): The box, chest, or container in which the Blessed Sacrament is reserved, or kept. The tabernacle may be placed in the sanctuary or in a special Eucharistic chapel or area. A lamp or candle is kept burning near the tabernacle as a sign that Jesus is present. The word *tabernacle* means "meeting place."

usher

(UH•sher): A minister of hospitality who welcomes members of the assembly to Mass and helps direct processions and collections.

vestments

(VEST•muhnts): The special clothing worn by the priest and some other ministers for Mass and other liturgical celebrations. The priest wears an **alb** (ALB), **chasuble** (CHA•zuh•buhl), and **stole** (STOHL). The deacon wears a **dalmatic** (dal•MA•tik) or an alb and a stole. The colors of vestments usually indicate the season of the liturgical year.

wine

(WYN): A drink made from grape juice that has fermented. At Mass the consecrated Wine becomes the Body and Blood of Christ. We may receive the consecrated Wine from the cup at Communion.